My Chinese New Year

Monica Hughes

Raintree

Chicago, Illinois

© 2006 Raintree
a division of Reed Elsevier Inc.
Chicago, Illinois

Customer Service 888-363-4266
Visit our website at www.raintreelibrary.com

Designed by Joanna Hinton-Malivoire and Tokay
Printed and bound in China by South China Printing Company

10 09 08 07 06
10 9 8 7 6 5 4 3 2 1

Library of Congress Cataloging-in-Publication Data
Hughes, Monica.
  My Chinese New Year / Monica Hughes.
     p. cm. -- (Festivals)
  Includes bibliographical references and index.
  ISBN 1-4109-0778-3 (hc) -- ISBN 1-4109-0783-X (pb)
  1. Chinese New Year--Juvenile literature. I. Title. II. Series:
Festivals (Raintree Publishers)
  GT4905.H84 2005
  394.261--dc22
                                    2004023084

Acknowledgments
The author and publisher are grateful to the following for permission to reproduce copyright material:
Alain Evrard/Lonely Planet Images p. **20**; The Image Works/Panorama/Yang Qitao pp **18-19**; TRIP
pp. **21** (A Tory), **23** (H Rogers); all other pictures Harcourt Education/Tudor Photography.

Cover photograph of a celebration meal, reproduced with permission of Harcourt Education/Tudor
Photography.

Every effort has been made to contact copyright holders of any material reproduced in this book.
Any omissions will be rectified in subsequent printings if notice is given to the publisher.

Some words are shown in bold, **like this.** You can find out
what they mean by looking in the glossary on page 24.

Contents

Getting Ready

We are getting ready for the new year. I am getting my hair cut.

We clean the house, too. Chinese New Year is fifteen days long.

5

At School

We make New Year's **masks**.

We listen to a
New Year's story.

Decorations

We hang a **scroll** outside our house. It is for good luck.

財
源
茂
盛
達
三
江

We put decorations inside, too.

9

Special Food

On the first day, Mom cooks vegetables for us.

They will bring us a
long and happy life.

New Clothes

On the sixth day,
we get new clothes.

Then, we visit our family and friends.

A Special Meal

We have a special meal with our whole family.

These are fried **dumplings.**

Happy Birthday!

We all celebrate our birthdays during Chinese New Year.

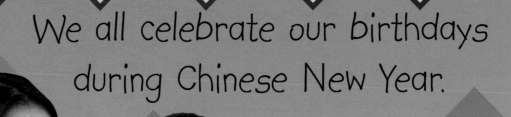

This is my birthday card.

We get red envelopes
with money inside.

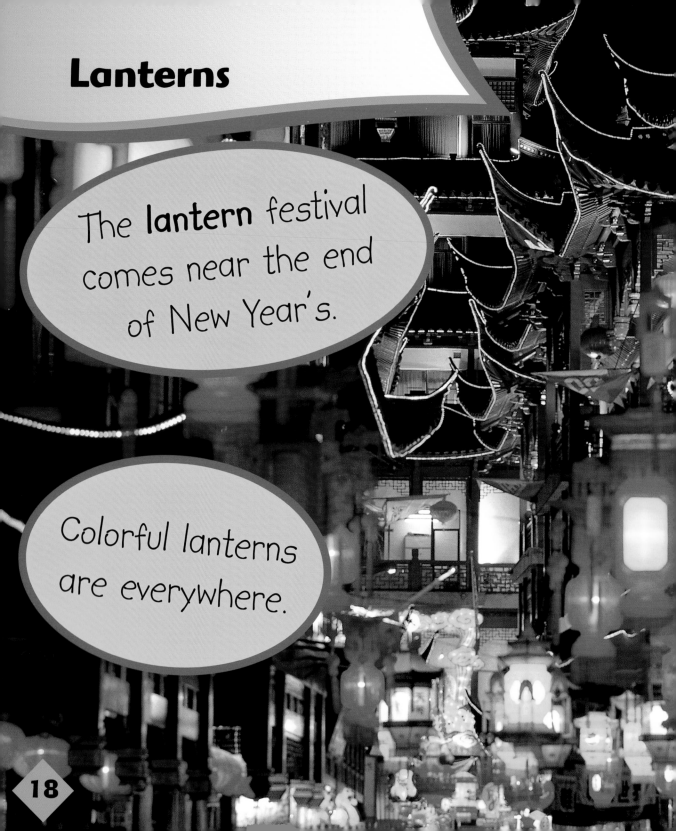

Lanterns

The **lantern** festival comes near the end of New Year's.

Colorful lanterns are everywhere.

18

We hang lanterns all around. Red is a lucky color.

19

Dragon Dance

This is a Chinese New Year parade. These men are doing a dragon dance.

Chinese dragons are not scary.
They are a **symbol** of power.

Fireworks

We are waiting for nighttime.

23

Glossary

dumpling Kind of wrapper made with rice flour, then filled with a food and cooked by steaming or frying

lantern light made by putting a candle or a light bulb inside a container, such as glass or paper

mask covering people wear over their faces. The Chinese believe that there is an animal for every year, so each year is named after an animal. For example, 2005 was the year of the rooster. Children may make masks of the face of the animal of the year.

scroll long, narrow poster with Chinese letters on it that is hung by a string at the top

symbol something that stands for something else

Index

10/26/06